Instructor

The
RESTORING
FATHER

(Studies in the Parable of the Prodigal Son)

Including
a study guide
for teachers and group leaders

• by William J. Richardson •

STANDARD PUBLISHING
Cincinnati, Ohio 39966

Quotations from *The Waiting Father* by Helmut Thielicke, translated by John Doberstein, translation © 1959 by John Doberstein, are here reprinted by permission of Harper & Row, Publishers, Inc.

Quotations from Dan Otto Via, *The Parables: Their Literary and Existential Dimensions*, copyright © 1967, are reprinted with permission of Fortress Press, Publisher.

Unless otherwise noted, all Scripture quotations are from the *New American Standard Bible*, ©1960, 1962, 1963, 1971, 1972, 1973, 1975, 1977, and are used by permission.

Cover picture by Wally Cochran.

Sharing the thoughts of his own heart, the author may express views not entirely consistent with those of the publisher.

Library of Congress Cataloging in Publication Data:

Richardson, William J., 1921-
 The restoring father.

 Bibliography: p.
 1. Prodigal son (Parable)   I. Title.
BT378.P8R53   1987   226'.806   87-6434
ISBN 0-97403-257-1 (Instructor edition)
ISBN 0-87403-258-X (Student edition)

Contents

Study Guide

Student Book

Introduction

This study guide has been prepared to assist you in leading a class or group discussion in studying Dr. William J. Richardson's *The Restoring Father: Studies in the Parable of the Prodigal Son.* For each chapter, discussion questions are provided to help you and your students dig deeply into the message of the third parable in Luke 15.

We recommend that you study the material on your own first. Study it not to prepare a lesson, but to understand and apply the principles to your own life. Use the space between the questions to make some notes as you wrestle with these principles. Then, once you have grasped the important principles enumerated in this great parable, begin to prepare to lead your class.

Be creative in the way you use the discussion questions with your class. At times, you will want the entire class to discuss a question together. At other times, however, you may find it more profitable to divide the class into smaller groups, especially if you have a large class. Assign the groups different questions and then have a spokesman from each group report on the discussion to the entire group. Or assign several small groups to discuss the same question and then use the reporting time to compare notes.

Sometimes, you will be given prompts in the space between the questions in this guide. In addition to using these prompts to guide your own thinking in your personal study, you can use the same prompts on a chalkboard or overhead transparency to direct the class. Create a large chart with answers given in group discussion.

We're convinced that there is a wealth of practical material in Dr. Richardson's study. It is our prayer that this guide will assist you and your group in mining that wealth and enriching your spiritual lives through this study.

Chapter One

The Greatest Story Ever Told

1. Unlike many of Jesus' parables, the parable of the prodigal son has more than just one lesson for us. The author points out that the lesson the student perceives to be the main message is the lesson that will generate the title he chooses to put over the parable. After reading this parable, give as many names as you can suggest for the parable. Read the beginning of chapter 1 in *The Restoring Father* for other names and compare. Which title do you like best? Why?

Names I thought of:

Names from the book:

The name I like best:

2. There are three parables in Luke 15. This one about a runaway boy is the third. Compare the three. What common message is in each? What ideas are in one that are not in the others? Do you think there is any special purpose for the order in which they were told?

Common message:

Unique ideas in the first parable:

Unique ideas in the second parable:

Unique ideas in the third parable:

3. What does this parable say about the relation of Jesus to the kingdom of Heaven? What does it say about our relation to the kingdom? What of our responsibilities within the kingdom?

4. Richardson quotes Thielicke and sums up the message of the parable this way: "You can come home." What do those words mean to you?

Chapter Two

The Nature of Sin

1. Richardson defines *sin* as being "out of relationship" with God: "seeking to establish [one's] life on his own terms apart from the father while using the father's resources." Accepting this definition, how would you say each son in this parable was guilty of "sin"?

Younger son:

Older son:

2. Using the above definition for sin, the goal when dealing with sin is restoration of the relationship. How does one maintain that perspective when he leaves the lesson and gets on with life? List some practical ways to be sure one's goal is restoration, and not mere punishment or vengeance, in the following areas:

Disagreements with a friend or spouse:

Parental discipline:

Church discipline:

Legal matters (civil and criminal cases):

3. Paul says, "Everything created by God is good, and nothing is to be rejected, if it is received with gratitude; for it is sanctified by means of the word of God and prayer" (1 Timothy 4:4, 5). Based on this, Richardson uses the term *distortion* to describe the result sin has in one's life. List some ways that sin distorts God's good creation. Then list some ways the child of God can avoid such distortions. (One example is cited below.)

Distortion	*Avoiding the Distortion*
Covetousness: When one covets some object, he begins to make it his god; he worships it by allowing it to become the most important thing in his life.	Avoid covetousness by taking care to see every object as created by God, and given to man as a means to serve God.

4. How do the terms *dead* and *lost* describe the condition of the sinner?

Chapter Three

The Meaning of Repentance

1. How is *repentance* different from *sorrow?* Cite some Scriptures to explain the difference.

2. How is repentance a positive attitude? Write a definition of *repentance* that expresses this positive, hopeful attitude.

3. How does one's understanding of repentance influence his attitude toward the preaching of the gospel? (Note Barton W. Stone's dilemma, cited in the text, that led to a change in his understanding.)

4. Do you think repentance is more past-oriented or future-oriented? Explain your answer.

Chapter Four

The Role of Obedience

1. Richardson says, "The son's return home did not create love and acceptance but was a necessary condition for its enjoyment." What do you think this says about the relation between our obedience and God's grace?

2. Read the following Scriptures on the necessity of obedience: Matthew 7:24; Acts 5:32; Romans 1:5; Hebrews 5:9; 1 Peter 4:17. Then explain why you agree or disagree with the following statements. (Note Richardson's dicussion of these statements in the text.)

"Obedience is necessary because of the nature of the gospel."

"Obedience is necessary because of the nature of faith."

"Obedience is necessary because of the nature of man."

3. Richardson says that obedience is "normal." Do you agree or disagree? Why? Read carefully the author's remarks under the heading, "Obedience as a Normal Response."

4. How do the parables related in Luke 17:1-10 and Luke 12:35-37 illustrate that obedience does not create grace? How does the response of each of the sons in the parable of the prodigal son illustrate the same fact? How does that fact affect your own obedience?

Chapter Five

The Nature of Grace

1. Richardson says that the father's primary and ultimate goal was not forgiveness, but restoration. What do you think of his analysis? What is the goal of God's grace?

2. The term *grace* is used both of God's favor extended to man (Romans 5:2) and the actions of Christians in response to God's favor (2 Corinthians 8:1). With that in mind, how would you define *grace*?

3. How did the father attempt to restore to his son the following relationships?

Fellowship with the father:

His identity as a son:

His place in the family:

4. How did the attitude of the older son threaten to thwart the goal of the father? What do you think would have happened if the older brother had seen the prodigal before his father did? What do you think that says of our responsibility toward other Christians today? Do you think there are some older sons today who thwart the grace of God in the lives of people? Explain your answer.

Chapter Six

The Prodigal Son
and the Principle of Restoration

1. Look at the following concepts. How does the parable of the prodigal son illustrate God's desire for each? Do you think it is fair to say that these three concepts adequately sum up Jesus' mission in life? Why or why not?

Reconciliation: bringing persons into a right relationship with God

Identity: bringing them into a right relationship with themselves

Community: bringing them into a right relationship with each other

2. How does the fact that there were New Testament churches before there was a written New Testament affect your understanding of how the New Testament should be used as a model for restoring the New Testament church today?

3. How do love and concern for the truth (Ephesians 4:15) correspond to the goals of unity and restoration of the New Testament pattern for the church? Which of the two is more apt to dominate in your own life? In your church? How can they be kept in balance?

4. Think of some situations in your own life or in your church that need the principles of restoration brought to bear. What can you do to bring about the needed restoration?

Situations   *Solutions*

THE RESTORING FATHER

The

Studies in
the Parable
of the
Prodigal Son

RESTORING
FATHER

·by William J. Richardson·

STANDARD PUBLISHING
Cincinnati, Ohio   39967

Quotations from *The Waiting Father* by Helmut Thielicke, translated by
John Doberstein, translation © 1959 by John Doberstein, are here reprinted
by permission of Harper & Row, Publishers, Inc.

Quotations from Dan Otto Via, *The Parables: Their Literary and Existential
Dimensions,* copyright © 1967, are reprinted with permission of Fortress
Press, Publisher.

Unless otherwise noted, all Scripture quotations are from the *New American Standard Bible*, ©1960, 1962, 1963, 1971, 1972, 1973, 1975, 1977, and
are used by permission.

Cover picture by Wally Cochran.

Sharing the thoughts of his own heart, the author may express views not
entirely consistent with those of the publisher.

Library of Congress Cataloging in Publication Data:

Richardson, William J., 1921-
    The restoring father.

    Bibliography: p.
    1. Prodigal son (Parable)   I. Title.
BT378.P8R53   1987   226'.806   87-6434
ISBN 0-87403-258-X
ISBN 0-97403-257-1 (Instructor ed.)

CONTENTS

Preface

These studies are built upon lectures given at Wi-Ne-Ma Week of Missions in Oregon in the summer of 1983 and upon the P. H. Welshimer Memorial Lectures given at Milligan College in the spring of 1984. I am grateful for the opportunity afforded me to develop these themes and the kindly reception given these presentations on both occasions.

My appreciation for the message of the prodigal son greatly increased during the thirty-one years I taught the "Life of Christ" to freshmen at Northwest Christian College. While we did not ignore critical questions in the study of the Gospels, our main emphasis was upon their message. Out of this experience came an enlarged conception of the scope of the implications of this particular parable for the understanding of the Christian faith today.

I am not unaware of the possibility of packing too much into the meaning and application of the prodigal son. I have sought to avoid this danger by paying attention to its fundamental themes before reaching out to understand its message in the larger scope of concerns that attract our attention today. In this, I trust I have achieved some success and that this short book will stimulate greater appreciation for the parable and its relevance for our time.

Chapter One

The Greatest Story Ever Told: The Prodigal Son Among the Parables of Jesus

This parable has been rightly described as a "pearl among the parables."[1] It tells a story with which the reader can easily identify, yet at the same time gives that story a twist that overturns generally accepted conceptions of what is proper in relations among persons. In turn, it challenges what often pass as orthodox conceptions of God and His attitude toward mankind. I am aware of the danger, when dealing with a parable such as this, of pressing it too far in the search for analogies. However, if the parable of the prodigal son does in fact deal with fundamental relationships—of God to man and of men to each other—the range of its applications extends beyond that of any other parable contained in the sacred record of Jesus' ministry. These studies reflect that conviction and seek to set forth some of these possible applications.

Before considering the message of the parable of the prodigal son, there are several important matters to engage our attention: what are parables, and what role do they play in the teaching and ministry of Jesus? What themes do they deal with? How are they to be interpreted? Of particular interest regarding this parable is the question whether there is a name it should be given that is more appropriate to its central theme. A number of suggestions have been brought forth, each deserving of special notice. Perhaps the most significant aspect of this parable is what it has to say about the person and mission of Jesus.

Our word *parable* derives from the Greek *paraballein*, "to place or throw beside." The basic idea is comparison. Hence, when some element from nature or from daily life is used to teach or to illustrate some truth about God or His kingdom, the comparison is called a parable.

We may distinguish several classes of parables. One, the similitude, draws upon typical, everyday situations, such as in the lost coin or lost sheep. Another is the so-called "example story," which does not depend upon drawing an analogy in order to apply its maxims because they are embedded in the story itself, as in the case of the good Samaritan and the Pharisee and the publican. A third type is the once-upon-a-time type of story, whose meaning depends upon the analogy drawn from the principal character or characters to the situation at hand. Obviously, the prodigal son belongs to this third class and is one of its most notable representatives.[2]

Parables may also be classified according to their subject matter. An examination of the views of some well-known scholars of this and an earlier era shows that, despite the variety in their classifications, their views reflect the fact that the underlying theme of all Jesus' parables is the kingdom of God. Some parables have as their principle objective to describe fundamental relationships in that kingdom, particularly as manifested in the life and ministry of Jesus. Other parables deal with the principles of conduct appropriate to the rule of God through Christ.

It is obvious from His extended use of parables and from the amount of space given to His parables in the Gospel accounts that Jesus attached great importance to this method of teaching. Why did He use parables so much? Why on this occasion, when Pharisees and scribes criticized His receptiveness toward sinners, did He respond to their grumbling by telling this story? Why did He not merely assert: "God loves and pardons sinners"?

He could have responded this way. Yet He chose the parable, and how forcefully and how beautifully did He deal with the issue they raised and at the same time get across a message concerning the nature of God. By this means, Jesus drew His hearers into a new understanding. God's love is not a proposition for debate but is, in Christ, a concrete reality in the realm of flesh and blood.

A parable may lead to spiritual insight in a way no discourse can. Hearers can identify with the story and the persons involved in it. The parable helps them to see themselves; it may, in turn, lead them to a decision. Helmut Thielicke relates an incident in the life of his son that illustrates how a parable may take hold of its hearers and lead them to insight about themselves.

> Some years ago I set my little son in front of a large mirror. At first he did not recognize himself. . . . He quite obviously enjoyed seeing the small image that smiled at him from this glass wall. But all of a sudden the expression on his little face changed as he began to recognize the similarity of the motions, and he seemed to be saying: "that's me."
>
> The same thing may happen to us when we see this story. We listen to it as if it were an interesting tale with which we ourselves have nothing to do. A rather odd but fascinating fellow this prodigal son. Undoubtedly true to life, undoubtedly a definite type of person we have all met at some time or other. And certainly we are all objective enough to feel a bit of sympathy with him.
>
> Until suddenly our face may change too, and we are compelled to say, "There I am, actually this is I."[3]

A. M. Hunter says that parables sometimes "contain the ambush of the unexpected." He quotes P. G. Wodehouse: "A parable . . . is one of those stories in the Bible which sounds at first like a pleasant yarn, but keeps something up its sleeve which suddenly pops up and knocks you flat."[4]

We see this in the prodigal son. Jesus was criticized for eating with sinners; and told a story which has a father performing the most undignified act that a father in that culture might do—running out to embrace his wayward son.

Our understanding of any parable should be guided by our awareness of the context, the situation that called forth the parable, and the intention of Jesus. However, once the truth of the parable is known, it may be broadened in its application, but these applications should still be controlled by its original intention and meaning.

A few of Jesus' parables, most notably the sower and the tares, are allegories. Each element of the parable has a point of application, and the relationship is so direct that the elements of the parable function as metaphors: "The sower sows the Word." "The field is the world." While other parables have qualities resembling the allegory, they generally have but one basic point of comparison to make to which other elements of the parable are subordinate. They may still, however, exhibit "allegorical traits." For example, some allegorization of the prodigal son is necessary in order to grasp the intention of Jesus on this occasion, but we should exercise care lest in the process of drawing comparisons, we commit the error of introducing a strange context to the understanding of the parable. I believe Tertullian was making this parable carry too much freight when he allegorized it in the following manner:

> The older son is the Jew, the younger son is the Christian. The inheritance which was shared is the knowledge of God which is man's birthright. The citizen in the far country who hired the younger son is the devil. The robe placed on the returning son is the sonship lost by Adam at the time of the Fall. The ring is the sign and seal of baptism; the feast is the Lord's Supper; and the fatted calf is Jesus.

The themes that Tertullian introduced to this interpretation are not themselves inappropriate to the Christian faith, but their projection into the interpretation of this parable is unwarranted.

We shall be giving further attention to how this parable is to be interpreted. Before doing so, we should consider what is the most appropriate title for the parable. Other titles have been suggested, each having something to commend it. Whatever our conclusion, we recognize that it is not likely that any title will supplant the one by which it has been commonly known.

The traditional title, the prodigal son, suggests that the younger son is the center of the story. Many would still see it so; they would prefer to call it the lost son in order to have the title coincide with the companion parables, the lost sheep and the lost coin, also found in Luke 15. Others call this the parable of the lost older brother. One writer referred to it as "The Other Prodigal," or "How to be a Prodigal Without Leaving Home." Ernst Fuchs calls this "The Parable of the Two Lost Sons"; each was lost in his own way, one in the "far country" and the other "behind a barricade of self-righteousness."[5] J. D. M. Derrett suggests the title, "The Recovery of the Unity of the Family." It is easy to appreciate

J. Jeremias' proposal, "The Loving Father," or Thielicke's, "The Waiting Father." The parable might also be appropriately called the running father; or, in view of the father's appeal to the older brother to join the welcoming celebration, the pleading father. In the light of the picture of the father it gives and of the prospects for life in the father's house, the parable could be called a parable of hope. There can be a homecoming because there is a home to come to.

There are good grounds for calling this the parable of the restoring father. The story throughout reflects the father's desire to restore the prodigal to himself and in the process to restore to him his true identity as a son. The father wanted also to restore brotherhood between his sons, and thereby to restore his family and its unity.

It is surprising that some have refused to identify the father in the parable with God or to allow even the simplest allegorizing in the interpretation of the parable. The context seems to demand that each of the persons of the drama be a point of reference for some aspect of the situation described by the gospel writer. In the context of Luke 15, we have the tax-gatherers and sinners, Jesus, and the Pharisees and scribes. The Pharisees and scribes murmur against Jesus because His association with tax-gatherers and sinners implied acceptance of them. Surely, then, there must be significance in the father, the older son, and the younger son of the parable. As Hunter writes, the only interpretation that "makes sense" of the parable "is that which identifies the father with God, the younger son with the publicans and sinners whom Jesus befriended, and the older son with the scribes and Pharisees who criticized him for doing so."[6] This approach to interpretation is reinforced by the fact that it appears alongside the parables of the lost sheep and the lost coin.

In their general outlines all three of these parables contain the same message: (1) something or someone was lost, (2) somebody cared, and (3) he rejoiced when the lost was found. The stated conclusion of the lost sheep and the lost coin must likewise be that of the lost son: there is rejoicing in God's presence when the lost is found.

Indeed, there is one principal point in this parable and it has to do with the father, whether we choose to speak of him as the loving father, the waiting father, the running father, or the restoring father. The love of the father is the theme that unifies the other aspects of the parable. The younger son was the prodigal, the squanderer. What did he squander? It was the father's patrimony benevolently bestowed in advance of the accustomed time. We have in the story a lost son or lost sons. What was their lostness? It was their separation from their father's love, a separation not necessarily dependent upon distance in geography. If we focus our attention upon the undignified running and pleading of the father, only the theme of love can account for the behavior and justify it. If this is a story of restoration, it is a restoration of sonship and brotherhood by the acts of a loving father. If this is a parable of hope, in what is that hope grounded if not in the love of the father? Moreover, since this main theme—the father's love—is "filtered" through the other persons in the parable, some analogies must be drawn from their situation in relation to the father; hence the need and justification for some allegorizing in our interpretation, provided that the allegorizing is governed by the intention of Jesus in this context.

Finally, this parable compels us to consider the issue of the nature and mission of Jesus (Christology). All the parables, in fact, do so, although not to the same degree; for in the parables, Jesus is speaking about some aspect of God's reign. Whether He deals with the coming of the kingdom, grace in the kingdom, life as a disciple in the kingdom, or the crisis of the kingdom, the question arises: what is His right to speak of such matters? In this particular instance, for example, what right does Jesus have to say what God's attitude is toward publicans and sinners? Implicit to the giving of the parable is an assertion of Jesus' authority and of Jesus as the one in whom God's forgiving love is embodied. Thus, Ernst Fuchs asserts, in a statement translated by Jeremias: "When a parable depicts the goodness of God, that goodness is actualized in Jesus. When a parable speaks about the kingdom, Jesus 'hides himself' behind the word Kingdom as its 'secret content.'" The parables are the "veiled christological self-attestation of the historical Jesus."[7]

In some parables, the relation of Jesus to the kingdom is most explicit. Consider, for example, the unfaithful stewards (Matthew 21). The owner of the vineyard let it out to stewards, then yearly sent servants to receive the fruit. However, these were shamefully treated and turned away empty. Finally, the owner determined to send his son, saying, "Surely they will respect my son." But the stewards conspired to kill the son and take the vineyard to themselves. Set in the context of passion week, this parable leaves no doubt about the identity of the son in the story and, therefore, of the relation of Jesus to the kingdom of God.

Although not as explicit as the unrighteous stewards, the prodigal son is no less clear in what it says about Jesus and his relation to the Father. Jesus has been accused of associating with and receiving sinners. This parable is His defense of himself and His mission, His answer to those who are offended by the gospel He preaches. But He defends himself and His actions by talking about God. How can He do so except on the basis of His claim to know God in a unique way and to have the right to extend forgiveness to sinners on God's behalf. This claim is reinforced by the conclusion of the companion parables, the lost sheep and the lost coin, where Jesus declares: "Even so, there is rejoicing in heaven over one sinner who turns again," a conclusion equally appropriate to the prodigal son. Jesus is saying, in effect, "I know the Father, and I know how He feels about matters of this kind!" When He speaks thus of God, He speaks also of himself. One cannot do justice to the parable of the prodigal son without considering what it implies about the nature and person of Jesus.

Helmut Thielicke expresses most eloquently the way that the claims of Jesus about himself are bound up with the message of hope in the parable of the prodigal son.

If this were just anyone telling us this story of the good and kindly Father we could only laugh. . . . But this is not just "anybody." This is Jesus Christ himself who is speaking. And he is not merely telling us about this Father; the Father himself is *in* him. He is not merely imagining a picture of an alleged heaven that is open to sinners; in Him, the kingdom is actually in the midst of us. Does he not eat with sinners? Does He not seek out the lost? Is He not with us when we die and leave all others behind? Is He not the light that shines in darkness? Is He not the very voice of the Father's heart that overtakes us in the far country and tells us that incredibly joyful news. "You can come home. Come home."[8]

Chapter Two

The Nature of Sin: "Into a Far Country"

A certain man had two sons; and the younger of them said to his father, "Father, give me the share of the estate that falls to me." And he divided his wealth between them. And not many days later, the younger son gathered everything together and went on a journey into a distant country, and there he squandered his estate with loose living.

Now when he had spent everything, a severe famine occurred in that country, and he began to be in need. And he went and attached himself to one of the citizens of that country, and he sent him into his fields to feed swine. And he was longing to fill his stomach with the pods that the swine were eating, and no one was giving anything to him.

Luke 15:11-16

It hardly seems necessary to talk about the nature of sin; everyone knows what sin is. Yet this parable provides a dimension for understanding the nature of sin that is often overlooked, a dimension that, in my judgment, is the most important aspect of this spiritual phenomenon.

The text declares that the father divided his wealth between his sons. The term used here for wealth is bios (life); he divided his life. This is not to suggest that money itself is life, yet one's property fittingly symbolizes the expenditure of one's time, energy, and talent and so may represent one's life, although it can never substitute for it. According to the custom of those times, a person might divide his property among his heirs during his lifetime, although the usual practice was to wait until death to do so. The normal procedure was that the eldest son, in such a case as this, would receive two-thirds of the inheritance, and the younger son, one-third. This reflects the operation of the law of the firstborn

17

(*primogeniture*). It was possible for the distribution to be made before the father's death, but the younger son could only sell the "right" to his share of the property, which would then be taken up by the buyer after the death of the father. The father could continue to receive the earnings (the *usufruct*) from that land during his lifetime. That is why the father still had something to give when the prodigal finally returned home.

So the younger son sold his "right" and with the money gained from the sale went off to a far country. But what was his sin? Several suggestions have been made. One is that of poor stewardship. Others have suggested that it was repudiation of the ruler of the household or a desire to be free from that ruler. An obvious suggestion is that his sin was wine, women, and song; he wasted his substance in riotous living.

The Basic Sin: Being Out Of Relationship

Sin is all these things and more. But there is something more basic than any of these. Whatever the conditions of life in the far country that may be called sin, there is a more basic condition, a more basic sin, that preceded them and was their cause. He sinned before he ever left home. His first and basic sin was the breaking of relationship. Note here the parallel between the lost sheep, the lost coin, and the lost son. Even though it is not called "sin," the basic problem in the lost sheep and the lost coin is being out of relationship. The goal in all three of these parables is to restore the relationship, the recovery of right relationship; this is why there was rejoicing when the sheep was found, when the coin was found, and when the son was found.

The basic sin of the son was this: he was seeking to establish his life on his own terms apart from the father while using the father's resources. He was, in effect, treating his father "as if he were dead."[9] The leaving home of itself was not sin, except insofar as it represented his separating himself from his father. This concept of sin is just as applicable to Eden (Genesis 3) as it is to the prodigal of Luke 15.

Langdon Gilkey, in his *Maker of Heaven and Earth*, relates the fact of sin to two affirmations about man associated with the original act of creation, which gave to man a distinctiveness not shared by any other creature on earth. (Note that the lostness of the sheep can never be attributed to sin as can the lostness of the younger son.) First, like all else in creation, man was made out of nothing. He is creaturely, therefore *dependent*. Secondly, man was made *in God's image;* hence he has a freedom that is real (though not absolute). He is at the same time *dependent, yet free.* This is why God—like the father in the parable—cannot compel man to use his stewardship properly or compel him to come back into relationship with himself when man is lost. The very endowment of freedom, which gives man his uniqueness, means he may abuse it. The time comes when the policeman must be on the inside. Fellowship cannot be compelled. Because he is dependent, man must "commit his security to some trusted power." He must exercise his freedom in the choice of appropriate goals to which he may commit himself. His wholeness consists in the unity of this *freedom* and this *creaturely dependence.* How does one get that unity? It comes by being in fellowship with God. For only in this relation to God is there freedom from the anxiety and terror of our time-bound existence. Only in this fellowship do we bring into balance the dependence that is our nature as created beings and the freedom that is our nature because we are made in His image. This is why the subject of the nature of God's authority is so important. He exercises his authority, not as a despot intent on displaying His power, but as a Father, and in such a way as to release us to the full participation in our being as persons made in His image.

But what if man is unwilling to "commit his security" to another, unwilling to live the life of dependence, and instead seeks to establish his own structures of security, to declare his independence from God, to become his own god? This is the basic Biblical conception of sin, and its results, in Gilkey's words, "are devastating for man's total being."[10] So many times in our talk about sin, we focus upon the symptoms rather than upon the root problem itself. It is not breach of the law as such, as serious as that is, but separation from God that is man's basic sin. Put in other terms, it is refusal to live the life of trust and commitment—refusal to acknowledge our dependence. Its result in life is disobedience to the law given to guide the life of faith.

Perhaps we can illustrate the above by the use of some simple diagrams. The basic meaning of sin *(hamartia)* is missing the mark, a meaning also conveyed by such related terms as *transgression* or *wickedness*. We may depict this concept by drawing a target with the arrow aimed at but falling short or wide of the target. The arrow has missed the mark.

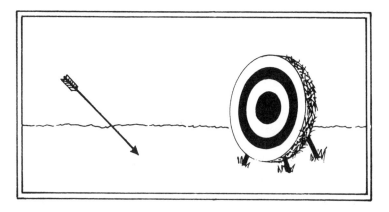

The question then is, "What is the mark or target?" On the one hand, we may see the target as the law, which is where most people stop in their consideration of the nature of sin. Sin, then, is any action—of thought or deed—that falls short or wide of the target (We often speak of it as failing to come up to the standard). In this case sin may be pictured as follows:

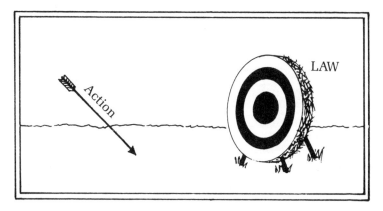

If the law presents the command: "Thou shall not covet," the avoidance of coveting becomes a target toward which to direct one's action; hence, if one covets, that act falls short or wide of the mark and so is sin.

The above is a legitimate way of understanding the nature of sin, as the experience of the prodigal subsequent to his leaving the father shows. But the same diagram may depict sin in a still more fundamental sense. Let the target now represent not just a norm set forth by law, but God himself; and let the arrow represent not merely an action, but life itself. If God is the source of life, He is also its proper goal. "Thou hast made us for thyself," wrote St. Augustine, "and our hearts are restless until they find their rest in thee." Hence, a life not lived in relation to God—a life without faith—is off target.

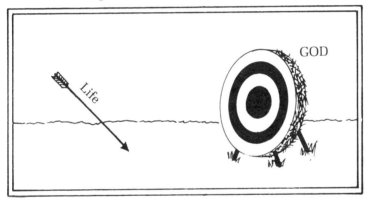

Sin, then, describes, not just wrongful actions, but the *whole life* not lived in relation to God. Thus, the sin of the prodigal, in seeking to establish his life on his own terms apart from his father, is the sin of mankind estranged from God.

Sin as Distortion of God's Gifts

What happens to life when it is off target is that it faces the threat of distortion at every point. Individual actions may still possess virtue or goodness and should be so acknowledged, but when the attempt is made to live life independently of God, the threat of distortion hangs over the way we use our God-given endowments, in the way we relate to

21

things, or in the way we relate to other persons. Thus, Helmut Thielicke describes the situation of the prodigal in this way, "Everything he has came from his father, but he uses it all *without* taking him into account." Where before he could use his father's gifts under the care and guidance of the father, he now faces the temptation—and succumbs to it—to use these gifts in a manner inconsistent with his father's nature and intention. His body and his possessions were both gifts, good things, but "as he uses them they become his undoing, for he uses them for himself, he uses them *without* the father."[11]

My choice of the word *distortion* to describe this result in life is based on the conviction that nothing created by God is evil in itself. It is important to believers to understand this because the spiritual life must not be built on the premise that either the body or matter itself is inherently evil. "Everything created by God is good, and nothing is to be rejected, if it is received with gratitude; for it is sanctified by means of the word of God and prayer" (1 Timothy 4:4, 5). What God created may be perverted, but it is not evil in itself. Evil consists either (1) in making the created thing a goal in itself, which is idolatry, or (2) in using the created thing in a manner not in keeping with God's creative purpose.

Effects of Sin

The further results in the life of the younger brother are no less tragic. He fell into bondage. He set out to be free, yet was in bondage. Again, I find Thielicke's description most helpful.

> He is *bound* to his homesickness, so he *must* amuse himself. He is *bound* to his urges, so he *must* satisfy them. He is *bound* to a grand style of living and therefore he *cannot* let it go. . . . *That's* what freedom looks like outside the Father's house—to be *bound*, to *have* to do this and that, to be under a *spell*, to be *compelled* to pursue the path he has chosen by an inexorable law.

The world sees the facade of the free autonomous person who defiantly asserts "I did it my way." But inside his heart the man who sets out to establish his life on his own terms apart from the Father "hears the rattle of the invisible chains in which he walks."[12]

Our text uses two terms to describe the condition of the younger son. "This son of mine was *dead* ... and was *lost*" (Luke 15:24, 32). Thus, the basic picture of sin given in this parable is one that involves first estrangement from the Father, a separation whose consequences are the kinds of sin spelled out by the law—the loss of stewardship and the perversion of human powers and capabilities.

Luke 15 and Romans 1 Compared

The prodigal son thus serves to illustrate the concept of sin and its consequences set forth in Romans 1:18ff. There is a striking resemblance between the message of the Romans passage concerning the nature of sin and that of Jesus' parable. Man's first sin, according to Paul, was not a breach of norms such as those described by law. His first sin was his separating himself from God, his breaking of his proper relationship with the Creator. (Note Romans 1:21-25.) Here Paul charges that although men already knew God, having perceived His "eternal power and divine nature ... through what has been made" (Romans 1:20), they did not honor Him as God, nor did they give Him thanks. They became "futile in their speculations" and "exchanged the glory of the incorruptible God for an image in the form of corruptible man and of birds and four-footed animals and crawling creatures." They substituted the worship of the creature for the worship of the Creator. All these represent a breach of their relation to God, a separation that preceded and led to the distortions men experienced in every part of life. These perversions are described in verses 24-32, and what Paul describes here are not qualities that are inherently evil. They are types of conduct that are abuses of some God-given human powers or capabilities—a distortion of the gifts God gave to man, whether involving relation to self, relation to others, or relation to things.

Three times in this passage Paul writes: "God gave them over" (Romans 1:24, 26, 28). He gave them over to their own self-determination and self-destruction, allowing them to experience the consequences of their way of life. He allowed them to lose their stewardship (verse 25); He allowed them to misuse their sexuality (verse 26); He allowed them to experience strife in interpersonal relationships (verses 28-31). In this view, sin as the distortion of true humanity is a form of punishment—the punishment man experiences as a consequence of his loss of fellowship with God.

Like the father of the prodigal, God never ceases to love and to long for His children. But for this very reason He does not deny to them the one quality that makes them fit subjects for fellowship, namely, their capacity to choose. And in granting to man that choice, God risks the threat of loss of fellowship.

Taking our clue, then, from the parable of the prodigal son and from Romans, we may define sin as seeking to establish one's life on his own terms apart from the Father while using the resources the Father provides.

The Sin of the Older Brother

But what of the older brother in the parable? Does he not also represent in his own way the same sin? Could one be alienated from his father without leaving home? To be sure, he did not go into "a far country." He did not separate himself in distance from his father. He could claim to have always been obedient (Luke 15:29). Like the Pharisees and the scribes, he had kept the law. Yet in spirit or attitude, he had left the father. He did not leave the father by moving away; he left him from within his heart. He, too, was seeking to establish his life on his own terms—on the basis of merit. His goodness was a means to an end. He was obedient, but for the wrong reason. He saw his obedience as having bound his father to him—as having placed his father under some kind of obligation. Is this the reason for living the life of faith? Is not the relationship itself the goal and the reward; or, as the older brother seemed to think, is the relationship a means of getting something else? Thus, out of his attempt to make his relationship with his father a matter of merit and reward, the other brother showed his heart to be as much out of tune with the father's as was that of the brother who took his father's patrimony and moved to a far country.

One can make an idol of his piety in whatever form it takes, like the Pharisee in the parable of the Pharisee and the tax-gather (Luke 18). The Pharisee's goodness was not an expression of gratitude, love, or trust. It was an effort to bind God to himself through his own merit.

What we see in the prodigal son is a younger brother "lost in a 'far country'" and an older brother "lost behind a barricade of self-righteousness."[13]

There is yet another important matter in this parable that must be emphasized. Even at the point where it contains features that are tragic, it presents several things about the lost son that are signals of hope. He had indeed sought to establish his life on his own terms independently of his father. Because of his separation from his father, he had experienced distortion at every point of his life, and he was in bondage. But this parable does not belong to the category of the tragic, and the above is only part of the story. The picture it draws of the son is that he is still capable of fellowship. He is still capable of making decisions—of choosing yet to be in his father's house. The memory of his father's love and care can still reach him. He can still respond to the word of grace: "You may come home; there is a home to come to."

Chapter Three

The Meaning of Repentance: "I Will Arise and Go to My Father"

> I tell you that in the same way, there will be more joy in heaven over one sinner who repents, than over ninety-nine righteous persons who need no repentance. . . . there is joy in the presence of the angels of God over one sinner who repents. . . . But when he came to his senses, he said, "How many of my father's hired men have more than enough bread, but I am dying here with hunger! I will get up and go to my father, and will say to him, 'Father, I have sinned against heaven, and in your sight; I am no longer worthy to be called your son; make me as one of your hired men.'"
>
> Luke 15:7, 10, 17-19

The sin of the prodigal son, which led to the other sins we associate with his prodigality, was in separating himself from his father, in seeking to establish his life on his own terms apart from his father. What the situation called for, then, was a decision to return to his father. He may well have regretted the misery into which he had fallen. What he needed now was the decision to leave that condition and return to his father. The New Testament term that best expresses the concept of decision is *metanoia*, which most translations render as "repentance."

Our thinking about *metanoia* has been strongly affected by the medieval concept of penance, and we have accepted that inheritance without sufficient criticism. A. T. Robertson, who taught so many years at the Southern Baptist Theological Seminary, writes: "It is a linguistic and theological tragedy that we have to go on using 'repentance' for *metanoia*." [14]

The concept of penance developed by the schoolmen of the twelfth century viewed it as the sacrament to deal with sins committed after baptism. It was regarded as the second plank thrown out to the sinner after shipwreck, the first plank being baptism. Hence, penance was not part of becoming a Christian, but was for the person already a member of the church, which, of course, included everybody considered a member of society. Penance was a fourfold process. It began with contrition (*paenitentia*,) sorrow for sin or aversion to sin; followed by confession of sin to the priest, a requirement to be fulfilled at least once a year. The third phase was satisfaction (*poena*) consisting of works regarded as penal in their design, as medicine for spiritual wounds, or as compensation. The final stage was absolution, which was pronounced by the priest. In this system, repentance was primarily sorrow for sin, and therefore had to do with the past. Insofar as it involved the will, it meant determination not to repeat an offense. In its main outline, this fourfold process is appropriate for sins committed by one already in Christ. The weakness of limiting the concept to sorrow for sin is that it fails to embrace what is involved when persons are making the decision to commit their lives to Christ, which is the meaning of *metanoia* when it is applied to that process—"repentance toward God" (Acts 20:21). Although we use the term "repentance" in this study, we recognize that it is flawed because of its association with past usage.

Repentance as a Change of Mind

Metanoia means a change of mind (attitude) and life. It is often, though not always, preceded by sorrow but is different from sorrow. Alexander Campbell used the term *repent* to translate *metamelomai* (regret) and the term *reformation* to translate *metanoia*. Some such distinction is called for in the case of the prodigal. He could have remained in the far country regretting the actions that got him there, despising the conditions of his existence, even abandoning the riotous style of life, and still not have made the decision that would bring him back to his father. He could have experienced regret and still not have done what the Bible talks about when it speaks of a change of mind.

There are in the New Testament different contexts in which repentance is called for: in the preaching of John preparing people for the coming kingdom (Luke 3); in the proclamation of the good news of Christ, in which people were urged to become His disciples (Acts 2); and in the life of Christians when they experienced failure (2 Corinthians 7:8-10). Although the actions called for differed in each of these contexts, they have in common the fact that in each case the persons addressed were called upon to have a change of mind, a change preceded by, and therefore distinguished from, regret.

This distinction between regret and change of mind is aptly reflected in Paul's remarks to the church at Corinth: "For though I caused you sorrow by my letter, I do not regret it .... [for] you were made sorrowful to the point of repentance" (2 Corinthians 7:8, 9). The distinction, and at the same time the relation, between regret and change of mind is further reinforced by Paul's next statement: "Godly sorrow brings repentance (*metanoia*)" (2 Corinthains 7:10, NIV).

Judas is a tragic illustration of remorse for the past—his betrayal of Jesus—without an accompanying change of mind that would have brought him back to Jesus (Matthew 27:3). The term used here to describe his state of mind is a form of the verb *metamelomai*—to regret, or to be sorrowful.

A further example of this distinction is Peter's sermon on the first Pentecost and the response it elicited (Acts 2). Peter concluded the sermon with the affirmation: "God has made Him both Lord and Christ—this Jesus whom you crucified" (Acts 2:36). His hearers were "pierced to the heart" (Acts 2:37); that is, they experienced conviction of sin and remorse. Then, in response to their query, "What shall we do?" Peter called upon them to "repent (*metanoesate*) and ... be baptized in the name of Jesus" (Acts 2:38). By repentance here, Peter could not have meant remorse for the past; they were already experiencing that. Repentance was an attitude toward the future, the decision to submit themselves to Jesus as Lord.

Repentance as a Positive Attitude

We may say the same of the repentance of the younger son; it was a change of mind toward home and his father. It was not a decision about the past but a decision about the future. His thoughts were not so much about what he was turning away from but of the place and situation he was turning toward. And despite any apprehensions he may have had about how he would be received, his attitude was basically positive; even the status of a hired servant in his father's house would be a joyous condition.

What produced this change of mind in the prodigal son? It is here that sorrow, regret, and remorse enter the picture. He had experienced the consequences of his choice of a way of life, and he had had enough of it. It had brought emptiness, bondage, loneliness, frustration, despair, indignity (a Jew reduced to becoming a herder of swine), and want (eating carob pods). But regret alone was not sufficient to produce this change of mind. The world is filled with people who are remorseful over the conditions of their lives but who will not make the decision that will change their lives. There was then still another element that led to this change in the prodigal and was essential to it; that was the memory of home and his father's love. Thielicke says that it was this element more than any other that robbed his life in the far country of any attractiveness it may have had and in turn induced him to repent.

Disgust with himself could never help him. It might perhaps have made a nihilist of him, but in no case would it have shown him the way back home. No, it's the other way round; it was because the father and the father's house loomed up before his soul that he became disgusted with himself ... a disgust that brought him home .... it was not because the far country made him sick that he turned back home. It was rather that the consciousness of home disgusted him with the far country, actually made him realize what estrangement and lostness is.[15]

Is there a lesson here for our concept of what our message is to the world? It is common today to think of repentance primarily as remorse and consider the way to produce conviction of sin is by preaching against sin. We live in the tradition of the Reformation where, with few exceptions, it was thought that the function of the law is to produce conviction of sin. Hence, the person outside, who may already have a sense of disgust about life, when he turns to the church hears only the word of judgment that thunders from the pulpit, whereas the Good News itself—with its vision of life in the Father's house—can produce a godly grief that in turn leads to repentance, the decision to arise and go to the Father (Acts 2:36-38).

Repentance and the Nature of Man

The call to change one's mind speaks profoundly about the nature of those to whom the command is addressed. It means they are capable of changing their minds. They can hear the call of God in the Gospel. They can get a vision of what life in relation to God, what life in the kingdom, can be. They can accept His judgment upon their present life in the "far country," and they can determine to do something about their situation. On the other hand, if man is so depraved as to have lost all will toward anything good, there is no meaning in issuing a call to repentance. Barton W. Stone, noted for his role in the western revival of 1801, tells in his autobiography about the dilemma he experienced as a revival preacher that led him finally to a different understanding about man's capacity to respond to the overture of God.

Often when I was addressing the listening multitudes on the doctrines of total depravity, their inability to believe, and the necessity of the physical power of God to produce faith, and then persuading the helpless to repent and believe the Gospel, my zeal in a moment would be chilled at the contradiction.[16]

If the story in Luke's Gospel were adapted to this style of evangelism, it would have called for some attempt to reach the prodigal while he was still in the far country in order to convince him of his hopeless and lost condition and of his inability to make any response unless enabled by his father to do so. Instead, it was his capacity for decision, ill-used at the first to bring him to lostness and death, that now became the means of his taking the faltering steps toward life. Dan Otto Via Jr. reminds us:

The prodigal did not blame someone else or the nature of life itself for his plight but rather accused himself and assumed responsibility for his situation.... What he accused was not an unalterable essence but an aspect of himself, a forgivable aspect.[17]

Insofar as this parable tells us anything about the nature of man, it reflects a concept of man as capable of grasping the vision of life in relation to God, of experiencing regret as he allows that vision to cast its light upon the present circumstances of life, and of choosing to put himself on the path that will bring him to the Father's house.

The repentance of the prodigal was the decision to be once again in relation to his father, to be in his father's presence—even at the cost of being in the status of an employee in the estate he once had spurned. The focus of that decision was not upon the past, what he wanted to get away from, but upon the future that lay ahead as he contemplated a life lived in relation to his father.

Repentance as an Attitude of Hope

Repentance then—properly understood—is an attitude of hope; and this parable must be seen as a parable of hope. To be sure, at the end, there is an unresolved element: will the older son come in out of the cold of his bitterness, his despicable insistence that repentance must be the long way back, that acceptance must not be easy. But basically the parable ends on a positive note. "This son of mine was dead, and has come to life again; he was lost, and has been found" (Luke 15:24).

Dan Otto Via, Jr. has examined the parables in the light of the classical types of drama—the comedy and the tragedy. The comedy is the drama that ends happily, while the tragedy depicts misfortune, catastrophe. Many of Jesus' parables are tragic, mainly the parables of the crisis of the kingdom, such as the talents, the ten maidens, the wedding garment. In the parables of the latter type, says Via, tragic action leads to a recognition scene and subsequent downfall and loss. But the story of the prodigal son is basically comic in the classical sense. The tragic action (separation from the father), leads to downfall. The recognition scene, however, has the father running out to meet and embrace his son; this is followed by the restoration: "Quickly bring out the best robe and put it on him, and put a ring on his hand and sandals on his feet" (Luke 15:22). This movement from death to life, which gives this parable its comic character, is one in which are combined the forgiving and restoring love of the father and the decision (repentance) of the prodigal to return home. He had exercised his freedom in the choice to turn away from his father; now he was exercising it in the choice to return home. The fact that there was a home to return to made that decision a decision of hope.

What a contrast with the mood that prevails in so many circles today. The twentieth-century view that sees man as a victim of necessity, as determined and not free, and which lacks the vision of the Father's house, can only see evil or tragedy as a normal condition of life. Why repent, why change one's mind? To do so would imply that there is some goal or object to be gained by the decision. Via describes this frame of mind as follows:

> Man [in the parable of the prodigal son] is seen as capable of recognizing who and where he is, particularly of knowing that something is wrong. This image of man provides a clear contrast with . . . the thorough going secularists. The semi-secularist may assert that life is painful and meaningless, but he is still protesting this state of affairs. He agrees with the prodigal at least in recognizing that something is wrong. The thoroughgoing secularist, on the other hand, has come to accept the normalcy of hell. He has given up the illusion that life ought to be meaningful and therefore has no protest to make. The loss of meaning is not wrong but rather normal. The prodigal is able not only to recognize that something is wrong but to resolve to do something about it.[18]

The regret of the younger son was real, as was his disgust with himself and his life in the far country. He had no merit. He no longer had a claim to make. Where before his demand was, "Give me," now he humbly prayed, "Make me." Home might never be the same; nor could the memory of the intervening years be erased from his mind. He probably even misunderstood what would be needed for acceptance, thinking that his return home might induce his father to love him. But the decision to return was a decision of hope.

Chapter Four

The Role of Obedience: "He Arose and Came to His Father"

"And he got up and came to his father."
Luke 15:20

As a story with a happy ending, the prodigal son necessarily focuses upon the forgiving and restoring love of the father. It is obvious from the story that his return home brought the prodigal to the enjoyment of this love. There is, therefore, in the movement of the younger son toward the father—as a type of obedience—an important lesson on the relation of human action to divine grace. Simply stated, that relation is this: the son's return home did not create love and acceptance but was a necessary condition for its enjoyment.

Throughout the greater part of the history of the church, there has been much dispute over the relation of human action to divine grace. Is salvation a process where God alone acts? Such would be the case if our answer were framed solely on the basis of the lost sheep or the lost coin. Is salvation a process where only human action has efficacy? Or is it a partnership consisting in an initiatory act on the part of God and an appropriate response on the part of the believer? If the son's return to his father may be regarded as a type of obedience, this parable will provide important insights into the nature of obedience and its role in the life of the believer.

The restoration movement has placed great emphasis upon obedience. It has recognized the importance of the question posed by the three thousand on Pentecost (Acts 2) and by the Philippian jailer (Acts 16): "What must I do?" This is fortunately not the unique emphasis of one movement. At the Third World Conference on Faith and Order, held at Lund in 1952, the delegates affirmed:

We believe that the revelation of God in Jesus Christ and the Scriptural witness to it are unique and normative for all ages. . . . We must always make sure in contending for our distinctive convictions that we distinguish between the confessions of the Truth to which we are committed and those expressions of it that were in part products of a particular age. If all denominations are prepared to do this in obedience to the Gospel alone, we may well come nearer to one another.[19]

How similar is this statement to that of Thomas Campbell:

With you we desire to unite in the bonds of an entire christian unity—Christ alone being the *head*, the centre, his word, the *rule*—an explicit belief of and manifest conformity to it, in all things—*the terms*.[20]

However, despite the virtue of the emphasis, it is still susceptible to several dangers. The chief of these is that we may misunderstand the meaning of obedience or its role in human salvation, the restoration of our humanity. What, then, is the relation of obedience in grace?

The Necessity of Obedience

Emphasis upon obedience is not an isolated phenomenon in the New Testament. We need to cite only a few examples:

Matthew 7:24—"Everyone who hears these words of Mine, and acts upon them, may be compared to a wise man, who built his house upon the rock."

Acts 5:32—"And we are witnesses of these things; and so is the Holy Spirit, whom God has given to those who obey Him."

Romans 1:5—". . . through whom we have received grace and apostleship to bring about the obedience of faith among all the Gentiles, for His name's sake."

Hebrews 5:9—". . . he became to all those who obey Him the source of eternal salvation."

1 Peter 4:17—". . . what will be the outcome for those who do not obey the gospel of God?"

The New Testament is replete with statements of this kind showing the necessity of obedience.

Obedience is necessary because of the nature of the gospel. The gospel is a proclamation about a person; hence, it requires a decision about that person. The proclamation, "God has made him both Lord and Christ," calls for a response, the acknowledgement of Jesus as Lord and commitment to Him.

Obedience is necessary because of the nature of faith. Faith is, of course, primarily a response to Jesus as a person. But the gospel also declares that in Christ God has elected, or chosen, us. Election, therefore, involves promise: we are elected to something. The gospel comes as a call to a relationship that involves a goal. There must be a response; we must commit ourselves to that call and to the goal that is implied in it. The Israel of the exodus was an elect community with a goal and attendant responsibility. In order to carry out the terms of the covenant, they had to commit themselves to carry out the goal of their election. Their failure to do so—their disobedience—is attributed to unbelief (Hebrews 3:13-19). Belief and obedience belong together.

Obedience is necessary because of the nature of man. We respond as whole persons. All the functions involved in our personhood are drawn into our response to some person or situation—our thinking, feeling, making an appropriate decision, and acting. For example, the response of the multitude on Pentecost was a response involving them as whole persons. The process as described in Acts embraced these elements: (1) fact—the gospel, (2) testimony—the proclamation of the gospel by Peter, (3) faith on the part of the hearers, (4) feeling, (5) action (obedience). This is the way people normally respond to a situation that they have either perceived themselves or have become aware of through the reports of others. This situation (reality), perceived or believed, evokes appropriate feelings and leads to appropriate action. We should expect that the response to the overture of God in the gospel should likewise be a response of the whole person.

Obedience as a Normal Response

We may say also that obedience is normal. The response for which the gospel calls does not invoke any powers or functions that are not part of our functions in everyday life.

There may seem to be a difference because of the import of the message. It is so momentous that it evokes a response that touches every part of our being and at a deeper level than any other message.

The effort to safeguard the vital part faith plays in our salvation has led some to minimize the role of overt actions in response to the gospel. This has had the unfortunate effect of suggesting that the gospel does not address itself to the whole person. In his *Christian System*, Alexander Campbell offers this response to those who assert that baptism is a "mere bodily act":

> We have been taught to regard immersion in water, into the name of the Father, the Son, and the Holy Spirit, as an act of the whole man—body, soul, and spirit. The soul of the intelligent subject is as fully immersed *into the Lord Jesus* as his body is immersed *in the water*. His soul rises with the Lord Jesus, as his body rises out of the water; and into one spirit with all the family of God is he immersed.

He then warns:

> Reader, be admonished how you speak of bodily acts in obedience to divine institutions. Remember Eve, Adam, and all transgressors on the one hand. Remember Abel, Noah, Enoch, Moses, Abraham ... on the other; and be cautious how you speak of bodily acts! Rather remember the sacrifice of a body on Mount Calvary, and talk not lightly of bodily acts. There is no such thing as outward bodily acts in the Christian institution; and less than in all others, in the act of immersion. Then it is that the spirit, soul, and body of man become one with the Lord.[21]

To illustrate in another way, benevolence is an action that involves the whole person, and could never be called a "mere bodily act." Note the elements that make up an act of benevolence as the response to another's need. Suppose the need is for food. What is involved first is the perception, or awareness, of that person and his need. This in turn evokes appropriate feelings, complex in nature, but consisting mainly of pity and compassion. The importance of compassion can scarcely be overemphasized; indeed to cast a loaf of bread to a hungry person without such an emotion would not be worthy to be called benevolence. But to be a total act of benevolence, the perception and the compassion toward the needy person must be completed by the hand holding out the loaf of bread. A total act of benevolence is a response of the whole person.

The same may be said of the process of becoming a naturalized citizen of another country. It is not a mere bodily act. The confidence one has in the new country and the feelings evoked by considering its advantages do not of themselves make one a citizen of that country. This mental state is completed in an overt act of publicly renouncing all former allegiances and committing oneself to the new allegiance.

Likewise, it was no "mere bodily act" for the prodigal to return home. He could have remained in the far country. While he was still there, he could have experienced remorse for the way of life that had brought his downfall. While he was still there, he could have changed his attitude toward his father and have changed the habits of his life. But as necessary as these were, they would not of themselves have restored him to his proper relation to his father. All the complex of elements that made up his state of mind required his return home for their completion.

Abraham as an Example of Obedience

The person most often cited by New Testament writers as an example of the obedience of faith is Abraham. He fitly illustrates what we have said about obedience. Abraham received a call and promise, in which God was preaching the gospel to him beforehand (Galatians 3:8), although not in the precise terms we are familiar with now. In this case, Abraham was like the prophets who "made careful search and inquiry, seeking to know what person or time the Spirit. . . was indicating as He predicted the sufferings of Christ and the glories to follow" (1 Peter 1:10, 11). Nevertheless, the message to Abraham was good news. It involved a concept of God so radically different from that of his Mesopotamian forebears as to be described as "an abrupt discontinuity."[22] It involved a new relationship to God as a person, and a call to cooperate in a plan to extend God's grace not only to Abraham and his family, but to all the families of the earth. The faith of Abraham in response to this call was a faith that required obedience. "By faith Abraham, when he was called, obeyed" (Hebrews 11:8). God's call contained a promise on which Abraham was to set his hope. Faith meant that he must give substance to that hope (Hebrews 11:1)—to live his life in terms of that promise, in other words, to be obedient. Moreover, Abraham's response to the call of God was normal, as would have been his response to anyone whose integrity he trusted. He heard, he believed, he acted on the promise of God. Finally, his response to the call of God involved his whole person. Faith meant for Abraham that he must gather his family, his flocks, and all other possessions, abandon Haran, and put himself on the road to the land of promise. Every relationship of his life must bear the imprint of his decision to stake his life on the promise of God. The invitation was addressed to the whole person; the whole person must respond to it.

Obedience as a Means of Enjoyment

It is proper to emphasize obedience. But there is a danger in this emphasis, the danger that we may come to think that by our obedience we create grace, that by our obedience we induce God to love us. I recall reading some years ago a tract outlining the steps one takes in his initial response to the gospel. When the author came to baptism as the culminating step of this process he wrote, "Now God changes his mind toward the sinner." He was forgetting the message of the cross; God changed His mind about sinners long ago, if indeed He needed to change His mind at all. If some act of man, however proper, can favorably dispose God's mind toward him, there is no longer any need for grace.

Luke records two of Jesus' parables that, although strikingly different, bear upon the relation of obedience to grace. In the one parable, the unprofitable servant (Luke 17:7-10), the slave is required to work all day in the field, then to prepare supper for the master before taking his own evening meal. "He does not thank the slave because he did the things which were commanded, does he? So you too, when you do all the things which are commanded you, say, 'We are unworthy slaves; we have done only that which we ought to have done.'" In the other parable, of the watchful servants

(Luke 12:35-37), the master takes note of the faithfulness of the slaves in filling their posts while he was away. Upon his return, the master will seat the slaves at his table, gird himself and wait upon them. These parables are alike in that in neither case do the slaves have a claim upon the master. Their obedience does not bind him to them in any way. The watchful servants shows that the master nevertheless honors the faithfulness of his servants by what would have to be considered a graceful act.

Alexander Campbell described the relation of obedience to grace in the following manner: "There are no conditions for the procurement of grace, but only conditions for its enjoyment." If we remember that the term *procure* means "to acquire" or "to bring about by contrivance," the statement is quite in keeping with Paul's assertion that "God demonstrates His own love toward us, in that while we were yet sinners, Christ died for us" (Romans 5:8). We can do nothing to procure such a love; any commands that are given must be seen, then, as means of enjoyment of it.

The attitude of the older brother in this parable stands in marked contrast to this understanding of grace. When the father came to plead with him to join the welcoming festivity he remonstrated: "Look! For so many years I have been serving you, and I have never neglected a command of yours; and yet you have never given me a kid, that I might be merry with my friends; but when this son of yours came, who has devoured your wealth with harlots, you killed the fattened calf for him" (Luke 15:29, 30). The father's reception of the prodigal flew in the face of the older brother's belief that by his obedience he could lay claim upon his father's love. One can well imagine the dismay of the father in hearing these words. He was not unappreciative of the older brother's obedience through the years. But for him, it was his love that bound him to his sons. Now the older brother was asserting that by his obedience, he had bound his father to him. Nor did the return of the prodigal create that love and acceptance. He may have thought in these terms as he journeyed homeward. He knew he had no claim on his father. He felt he had forfeited his sonship. He may well have thought he needed to overcome the hostility his father must surely feel toward him, to dispose his father once again to love him. If such was the case, he was forgetting that his father had never stopped loving him nor been unwilling to accept him.

His return home—his obedience—did not change his father's mind; it did not create love and acceptance. But his return home was necessary in order for him to enjoy that love and acceptance and to be restored to the status his father wanted him to have.

Chapter Five

The Nature of Grace:
The Restoring Father

But while he was still a long way off, his father saw him, and felt compassion for him, and ran and embraced him, and kissed him.

Luke 15:20

No parable has so many names suggested for it as the parable of the prodigal son, each with some claim to validity. We should note, however, that what scholars judge to be the central theme of the parable affects their determination of the validity of the various titles. For example, Dan Otto Via, Jr. asserts this is "the son's story. His experience gives the plot its formal shape. . . . in the Prodigal Son the son not only gives the plot its structure but also initiates the action."[23] In this perspective, the possibilities for naming the parable are limited to the traditional prodigal son or the lost son. Titles calling attention to attributes of the father, while they may appropriately describe his actions, do not properly identify the parable.

On the other hand, Helmut Thielicke, expressing a view shared by A. M. Hunter, Joachim Jeremias, and others, contends that this is the father's story. "The ultimate theme of this story, therefore, is not the prodigal son, but the Father who finds us. The ultimate theme is not the faithlessness of men, but the faithfulness of God."[24]

To this point in these studies, I have utilized most often the traditional title in referring to the parable. My own conviction, however, is that the central theme of the parable is the father and his love. I believe this view is borne out by the position this parable occupies in Luke 15 along with the lost sheep and lost coin. All three of these parables share certain characteristics: lostness, caring, finding, and rejoicing. It is

43

clear from Luke's presentation that it was Jesus' object in all three parables to call attention to the rejoicing of God over the repentance of a sinner; it was the caring that led to rejoicing when the lost was found. The prodigal son shares this quality along with the others; therefore, the father's caring must be central to the story. I have also followed Hunter and others in identifying the "*dramatis personae*" of the parable with the parties in the context of Luke 15:1, 2: Jesus (as representative of God), publicans and sinners, and the murmuring Pharisees and scribes. For this reason, I see no need to restrict our usage to those titles based on the view that the father's love is the main theme of the parable. It is legitimate to make use of any titles that call attention to the way the other *dramatis personae*—the younger and older sons—fill out the picture.

Thielicke shows great insight in calling this parable the waiting father. Luke 15:20 states that "while he was still a long way off, his father saw him." It may be that this means nothing more than that the father was in the field examining the growing grain, looked up, saw the son, and ran out to greet him. But the text suggests something more. For quite some time, the father had been engaged in waiting, observing travellers on the road, hoping to see the familiar face of his son. He had a robe put aside in anticipation of this very day.

Those who complain of the fact that the father, unlike the shepherd in the parable of the lost sheep, had not earlier gone after the son, must be reminded that fellowship cannot be created or maintained by compulsion. But, although limited in what he could do by his love and desire for fellowship, the father still was not passive. He was anxious, hoping, looking, waiting.

The waiting father became the running father, he "saw him and felt compassion for him, and ran." Such haste "was beneath the dignity of a head of a family;" hence, it reflects the depth of his love.[25] But he cast aside any concern he may have had for his dignity. He was also taking a risk. His running might be seen as indulgent, encouraging the son's profligacy. In addition, he risked offending the older son. He was willing to take these risks.[26] Note the order of events: he embraced and kissed him; he interrupted the son's *mea culpa* speech by calling for the robe, the ring, the shoes, and the feast of celebration.

In his actions, the father typifies the grace of God. His grace functioned first in an act of compassion, forgiveness, and acceptance. We must remember that forgiveness does not mean that no sin was committed. While forgiveness is an act of grace, it is equally an act of judgment; and to accept forgiveness is to acknowledge one's need of it. The prodigal was correct in saying, "I am no longer worthy to be called your son" (Luke 15:21). But the father in his love did not accept this estimate, nor does the grace of God. "God demonstrates His own love toward us, in that while we were yet sinners, Christ died for us" (Romans 5:8).

But forgiveness was not the primary or ultimate goal of the father, or of God. He had a still larger objective in view to which forgiveness was a means. That objective was restoration. Hence, although lacking the euphonic quality of such titles as loving father, waiting father, running father, this parable may appropriately be called the restoring father; such a name fitly represents the father's goals in this situation. First, he wanted to restore the son to relationship (fellowship) with himself; he wanted the son to be reconciled (2 Corinthians 5:19). He wished also to restore to the prodigal his identity as a son; it was loss of this identity that the parable describes by the words *lost* and *dead*, while its recovery is described by the words *found* and *alive*. His sin, as we have seen, was his abandonment of his father; the goal of forgiveness was the restoration of fellowship and sonship.

But the removal of the prodigal had resulted not only in a broken relation with the father; it had also brought a breach in the relation between himself and his brother. Hence, a third goal of the father was to restore the family. The father was as concerned about the reconciliation of the brothers to each other as he was for the reconciliation of the prodigal to himself. There is probably no greater pain to parents than that of the estrangement of their children from each other; how much more must it cause pain to God to see estrangement in His family. This goal—the restoration of the family—explains why verses 25-32 are in the parable. The context, of course, required it as part of Jesus' answer to the grumbling of scribes and Pharisees. But more importantly, it was not just the relation of the father and the wayward son that was at stake; it was relations within the family. The structure and unity of the family had suffered distortion and needed to be restored. The same might be said of the church as the family of God today. Restoration of that family and its unity is a valid project. We shall say more about this later.

Meaning of Grace

Few words are so varied in application as the term *charis* (grace). Basically the term denotes a personal quality, sweetness, charm, or loveliness that produces delight or pleasure. From this meaning derive the several other meanings attached to *charis* in the New Testament. It may mean goodwill, loving-kindness, the kindness that bestows upon another what he has not deserved; in other words, favor extended without regard to merit. Again, it may be used to refer to what we have in our lives because of the goodness of God. Thus, Paul writes: "Through [Jesus] we have gained access by faith into this grace in which we now stand" (Romans 5:2, NIV); and "I thank my God always concerning you, for the grace of God which was given you in Christ Jesus" (1 Corinthians 1:4). The term may also apply to the attitude and actions of believers in grateful response to the loving-favor of God; thus, Paul can refer to the generosity of Macedonian believers in helping famine-stricken Judeans as *charis* (grace). In summary, grace describes the being of God; as Martin Luther used to say: "Grace is what God is." It also describes God's acting out of his deepest being. "For the grace of God has appeared" (Titus 2:11); grace is sovereignty surrendered. Finally, grace describes the fruit of God's action in human life as it evokes in its recipients the attitude of thankfulness. The younger son could not earn his way back. He was not worthy, and he knew it. He was received solely on the basis of grace. But once received back, once restored to the status of a son, he must live the life of a son—in stewardship. The freedom of sonship, now his as a gift, still meant he must be responsible. Applied to the life of believers today, this is the basis of Christian ethical action. "Religion is grace, ethics is gratitude."

We may need to remind ourselves that the father was still able to give to his son. He could not give the inheritance;

that was committed. But the income from the land was his until his death, and of that he could still give to his younger son.

We have been referring to the waiting father, the running father, the restoring father. Our thought turns now to the older brother: What if he had been the one looking, waiting, running?

His attitude was one of outrage; upon hearing of the welcome given his brother, "he became angry, and was not willing to go in" (Luke 15:28). He was like those of Thielicke's description, "'good people' whose religion never makes them really warm and happy."[27]

Why his anger? It resulted from a misunderstanding of the meaning of obedience. He saw commands as burdens to be borne, to be carried on one's shoulders (Is this why God gives commands?) rather than as means of expressing his identity or carrying out the implications of life in relation to his father. With such an attitude, he failed to see that commands are designed to help us to avoid distortion of our human powers and capabilities. He may actually have envied the life of wine, women, and song his brother "enjoyed." Moreover, he felt that his obedience had gained him merit that should have been recognized. The way for the father to honor his goodness was to reject the younger brother, or at least to make his way back *long* and *hard*. "You have never given me a kid" (Luke 15:29) is the angry protest of one who believed his obedience had put the father in debt to him—a debt now to be paid by the harsh treatment of the sinning brother.

Why do we obey God? Is it for the returns it brings? Is not the relationship itself its own reward? This was the attitude of the psalmist: "His delight is in the law of the Lord, and in His law he meditates day and night" (Psalm 1:2). One can obey God for the wrong reasons, or more correctly, one can keep the commandments for the wrong reasons; I am not sure that keeping commandments and obedience are the same thing.

Note how the older brother expressed his anger. Where the father said, "your brother" (Luke 15:27), the older son would only refer to the prodigal as "*this son of yours . . . who has devoured your wealth with harlots*" (Luke 15:30).

Like Jonah at Ninevah, he was wroth because the repentance of the sinner had been accepted.

Now it was the attitude of the older brother that threatened to damage the familial relationship. At its conclusion, the parable becomes the story of the entreating father. The father loved the older brother and appreciated his faithful service. Now he pleaded with him not to reject the gift of a reunited family, which, because of his grace and the prodigal's repentance, was possible again.

The result of his outrage was that it took the older brother away from the father. Where the younger son had left the father "by going away" the older son left him "from the inside."[28]

The lesson here for each of us is this: Whom God accepts as a child, I must accept as my brother. If I cannot rejoice when the Father rejoices or sorrow when He sorrows, my heart is beating "out of time with the Father's."[29] The older brother was making himself a stranger in the very house he was to inherit, which leads Thielicke to observe: "What a wretched thing it is to call oneself a Christian and yet be a grumbling servant in the Father's house."[30] Again, what would have happened to the prodigal if his older brother, in the state of mind we have been describing, had got to him first? The guilt the younger brother felt would have been magnified. Any feelings of hope he may have had would have been dashed to the ground. By the time his brother had finished with him, he would probably have kept on going down the road—down and ever down.

Each of us must be aware that we are the older brother to someone. And it is our task, when that person comes to us, to see that he gets on to the Father. The late Jack Sutton used to tell of the experience of a young divorcee, anxious to put her life back together after the tragic failure of her marriage. She visited a Sunday-school class one day where a sincere but misguided teacher expressed the conviction that there is really no hope for divorced persons; and it was in that mood that the young lady left the church that day. She had got to the older brother first, and he had failed to take her on to the Father!

But let us look now at the father. It might well be said of him: "Grace was what the father was." We need dwell only a moment on what the scenario would have been if the father's actions had corresponded to the picture often drawn of God. The father upon seeing the son's approach retreats to the house, bolts the door, and assumes a stance of nonchalant detachment as the son in tears pleads for admission and reinstatement. After an appropriate interval, he finally unbolts the door to allow his son to enter.

One might also picture a stern father, standing in the doorway, arms folded, demanding to know how the wayward son could assume the right to come back, or asking what he had done now to deserve such a reception.

Rather, the picture drawn is that of the waiting father, day after day scanning the horizon in the prospect that one of the faces among those making their journey along the road might prove to be that of his son, and again and again experiencing the disappointment of unrequited hope. And then came this day—a day marked by change not only for the prodigal, but for the father as well—it was his son's face that he saw. He now became the running father, who embraced and kissed his son, called for the robe, the ring, and the shoes, signals of forgiveness, acceptance, restoration to his status as a son. The lost was found; the dead was alive.

The question left unanswered in the parable is this: will there be a restoration of the family? The parable ends with the older brother astride the barnyard fence, outraged at his father's reception of the prodigal.

We must ask again where Christ fits in the parable. Here we distinguish two contexts. First is the original context in which Jesus delivered the parable, as preserved in the third Gospel. But there is also the context of the church when the parable was committed to writing by Luke, the post-Easter, post-Pentecost context. In the original context, Jesus fits into the parable in two ways. First he claimed authority to speak for God. He had been criticized for His association with sinners. In his defense, He told the story of the loving father, who is God. Thus, the very telling of this story was a Christological affirmation: "I can speak about God." Also, Jesus exhibited in His own life the compassion and forgiveness of God. "The kingdom of God has come upon you," He declared (Matthew 12:28). He ate with sinners; He sought the lost. "That is what the kingdom is all about!" But let

49

us look at the prodigal son in the light of Easter and Pentecost, which readers of the Gospel have the privilege of doing, and which they need to do in order to grasp its message for our day. In this perspective, two dimensions are added for our consideration: (1) Jesus is our elder brother (Hebrews 2:11-14), (2) In the cross of Christ, "God demonstrates His own love toward us, in that while we were yet sinners, Christ died for us" (Romans 5:8). Here are two dimensions that could not have been given to the story in its original context. But once we have done justice to the story in its original context, its message takes an added meaning for us in the light of our post-Easter perspective. Our true older brother is out there on the road scanning the horizon to see whether his younger brother is coming home, with the same love, the same longing, and the same compassion as that of the Father. He does so with this intention—to lead the younger brother to the Father. "For the Son of Man [came] to seek and to save that which was lost" (Luke 19:10). This intention carried him to Golgotha.

"And I, if I be lifted up from the earth, will draw all men to Myself" (John 12:32).

Chapter Six

The Prodigal Son
and the Principle of Restoration

"His father came out and began entreating him."
Luke 15:28

The idea of restoration has had a long and interesting history. From before the Reformation era to the present, and from within a spectrum so broad as to include Anabaptists on the one hand and Roman Catholics such as Hans Kung on the other, persons or groups have arisen to declare their commitment to this principle. These movements have seldom had the same perception of what aspects of the faith and the forms of its expression are to be subjected to the principle. However, they have generally shared in common the appeal to an earlier age that in their judgment more truly represents the genius of the religion of Christ—to which followers of Christ must be faithful. Does the parable of the prodigal son reflect the working of this principle? In turn, does the parable suggest a model of restoration that speaks to this concern today?

Asking a parable to serve as a model of restoration exposes one to the danger of making the parable say more than Jesus intended. A parable represents figurative speech. Can such a style of speaking yield the exactness of meaning implied by the term *model*? The propriety of this procedure may also be questioned on the ground that a parable should not be allegorized, that only one point for its meaning should be sought. Moreover, the idea of restoration as it has been popularly conceived seems too far removed from the intention of Jesus in the context where Luke places the parable. Is it reasonable to seek a paradigm of restoration of New Testament Christianity in a parable given to defend Jesus' association with publicans and sinners?

There is, I believe, justification for allegorizing some elements of the parable. I concur with Hunter in his contention that we have no other option in interpreting this parable than to identify "the father with God, the younger son with the sinners whom Jesus befriended, and the older son with the scribes and Pharisees who criticized him for doing so."[31] If, then, the *dramatis personae* of the parable are representative, as Hunter suggests, we may take seriously the intention of the father concerning relationships in his family as indicative of the intention of God concerning relationships in His household.

The underlying reality of this parable, as of most of Jesus' parables, which in turn gave structure to Jesus' ministry, is the kingdom of God. Indeed, it is possible to classify all the parables, as Dodd, Hunter, and others have done, according to the different aspects of the reign of God they illustrate. But as a theme, the "kingdom of God" is rooted in a still deeper reality: (1) God's bid for fellowship; (2) the acts of God, supremely in Christ, to recover man and bring him to fellowship; (3) the structures or relationships that characterize and express that relationship. In other words, restoring mankind to God and His kingdom, restoring relationships within that kingdom, and restoring modes of life in keeping with those relationships is the presupposition, whether explicit or implicit, of all Jesus' parables. Hence, as the one who brings the kingdom, and as the Lord designate of the kingdom, Jesus engaged in a ministry that involved three concerns, all reflected in the parable of the prodigal son. First, He sought to bring persons into right relation to God. Second, as a corollary to the first, He sought to bring them into participation in their identity as made in God's image. He came "to seek and to save the lost." Here it must be remembered that the term *sozo* (to save) means to restore to wholeness. We are not whole until we are in proper relation to God. Third, He sought to bring persons into community. He gathered about himself those who accepted His summons to discipleship and participation in the kingdom. "Do not be afraid, little flock, for your Father has chosen gladly to give you the kingdom" (Luke 12:32). All these concerns, as expressions of grace, are clearly exhibited by the father in the prodigal son—the recovery of his son to relationship with himself, the recovery of the identity of the son (dead but now alive, lost but now found), and the recovery of relationships within the family. This fact makes this one of the most comprehensive of Jesus' parables in the scope of its teaching. This accounts also for the fact that it may appropriately bear so many titles. To the extent, then, that the parable of the prodigal son reflects this deeper reality—God's seeking to reconcile persons to himself and to reconstitute His family— it is a model of restoration.

Problems in Understanding Restoration

How, then, does this parable function in the situation today where restoration has been declared to be both untenable and divisive? A generation ago, in the heyday of the Biblical theology movement, the plea for New Testament Christianity seemed to be the wave of the future. There were, of course, the differences in ways of expressing Biblical faith that one might expect from voices speaking out of so many backgrounds, but they shared in common the conviction expressed at Lund in 1952, that "the revelation of God in Jesus Christ and the scriptural witness to it are unique and normative for all ages," a statement that rather typically represents much of the tenor of the Faith and Order Movement in its first four decades.

Nevertheless, the concept of restoration has been deemed untenable. This appraisal is rooted in several developments. From one side was that approach that sought to find the essence of Christianity in some kind of experience, whether mystical, ethical, or intellectual, detached from any affirmations about Jesus of Nazareth. At best, He was a prophet, a reformer of Judaism, or an ethical model—an example to be followed rather than the mediator who could bring persons to the Father. The effect of this approach, in the words of Georges Florovsky, was "to disentangle Christianity from its historical context and involvement."[32] Hence, in this view, no appeal to a norm arising out of an earlier period could be tenable.

From the other side, the indictment of restoration was the response to inadequate conceptions of what restoration means. The failure to distinguish between the New Covenant itself and the Scriptures embodying it led to the conception of the New Testament as having been written for the express purpose of being a pattern. If taken seriously, this conception implies that the written New Testament preceded and produced the church, which is not historically true. The church was indeed produced by the New Covenant, and the written New Testament is our only authoritative source for knowing it. However, that covenant was in place (Matthew 26:28; 2 Corinthians 3:4-6; Ephesians 2:19, 20, 3:5) before the Scriptures embodying it were written. Lack of clarity on this point had the unfortunate effect of encouraging rejection of the very idea of restoration. As a corollary of viewing the written New Testament in this way, there developed a static conception of the church in which, without differentiation, all the elements of the life of the first-century church were taken as patterns for the church of today. This made even more difficult the task of delineating those features of the church of the first century that were cultural and relative from those that were permanent. In addition, the notion, often held, that the first-century church was perfect in the quality of life confirmed to the minds of many that proponents of restoration had not seriously examined the very materials they considered normative.

Restoration has also been seen as divisive. Viewed in one sense, this criticism has little, if any, merit. Any appeal to standards is divisive in that it separates those who receive the standards from those who do not. In this sense, the platform of the Lambeth Quadrilateral—(1)the Apostles and Nicene Creeds, (2) the Old Testament and New Testament Scriptures, (3)the two sacraments, (4) the historic episcopacy—is divisive. So also is the appeal of "Catholic" type churches to the evolved structure of the church in the second century as normative. Even Winfred E. Garrison's well-intentioned proposal to ground Christian unity solely in the confession, "Jesus is Lord," excludes from consideration those who do not make that confession.

At the same time, there have been attitudes associated with restoration that are divisive. Chief among these is making restoration a goal in itself, either placing it above concern for unity or excluding concern for unity altogether. At the very outset, we should note that such an approach overlooks a basic fact of existence for the church: unity is one of the identifying marks of the church. The church will not be fully restored until it is united.

Equally tragic is the effect in human relations of making restoration only the goal. The New Testament affords the example of Jesus, who combined grace and truth in His disclosure of God to us (John 1:14-17). Paul urges believers to behave toward each other the same way, "speaking the truth in love" (Ephesians 4:15). These two attitudes, love and the concern for truth, correspond to the twin goals—unity and restoration. The appeal to restoration reflects the commitment to truth; the appeal to unity reflects the commitment to love. Therefore, to make restoration only the objective is in effect to opt only for the commitment to truth and a tendency to overlook the demand that love makes in our relation to fellow believers. To appeal only to the norm (restoration only) breeds a spirit like that of the older son in the parable, who regarded his obedience as a mark of achievement and used the norms of that obedience as grounds for rejecting the brother, whom his father had accepted.

The Prodigal Son as a Model of Restoration

How, then, does the parable of the prodigal son relate to the question of the validity of the principle of restoration? Does it supply insights to help us improve our understanding of that principle and our articulation of it? Can the parable speak to the question of what should be the attitude of those who advocate the principle? There are four assertions that can be made in response to these questions.

1. On the one hand, the idea of God's seeking man for fellowship is so fundamental to Biblical faith that it is hardly necessary to seek specific warrant in Scripture for the principle of restoration. However, the parable of the prodigal son reflects positively the validity of restoration properly understood. The father seeks to restore the younger son to fellowship with himself, although limited in his action by the necessity of respecting the son's freedom. He seeks also the restoration of the structures and functions appropriate to that fellowship—recovery of the prodigal's identity as a son and recovery of the stewardship belonging to that identity. Put another way, the father in love seeks to overcome

the distortions that threaten life when it is not lived in terms of one's true identity: (1) distortion of the self and its endowments, natural and given, (2) distortion of one's relation to others, and (3) distortion in one's use of things.

Another structure the father seeks to restore is the family. He is as concerned about the reconciliation of the brothers to each other as he is about the reconciliation of each to himself. He cannot, of course, recreate the situation as it was before the younger son's leaving, but he can seek to restore the family, open still to possibilities for the future.

The obvious weaknesses of the blueprint model noted earlier does not nullify the use of the concept of pattern in applying the message of the prodigal son to the church today. We legitimately speak of patterns in human relationships—parenthood, brotherhood, and other societal relations. In this parable, the relation of the father to the two sons and their relation to each other are important structures. And while these relationships should not be viewed as mechanical, they are structures nevertheless, and not without normative significance to the church as the family of God. There are certain identifiable marks that make an association of persons the household of God (Ephesians 2:19) and differentiate this society from other associations; and since structure and function are inseparably related, the church must be faithful to its identity in order to accomplish its mission.

2. Participation in these structures should be regarded as a gift to be received in gratitude. Obedience, however necessary, is not achievement. As we have seen, the return of the prodigal did not create his father's attitude of acceptance but was necessary to his enjoyment of it. His repentance showed his readiness to fulfill any role his father might have for him. On the other hand, the older brother was a legalist; he viewed obedience as a means of achieving acceptability. The appeal to norms does not of itself make for legalism. Legalism is viewing obedience to norms as the ground of one's acceptance. If not a denial of grace, this attitude at least obviates the need for grace.

It is appropriate that a restoration movement emphasize obedience. But obedience must not be seen as achievement, as placing God in our debt, but rather as reception.

3. The attitude of the older son in the parable demonstrates also the need to combine the appeal to norms with the attitude of love. We have already considered what would have been the result if the older son, who always kept his father's commands, had reached the returning prodigal first. Dealing with people in terms of love does not mean the abandonment of standards. Indeed, the offer of forgiveness, as an expression of grace, is itself a judgment; it upholds the standard. The exultant cry of the father, "My son is alive . . . my son is found!" is a cry of grace, but it is also a judgment; for the son was lost and needed grace. Seeking the restoration of the son, as an expression of grace, is at the same time a judgment of his need for recovery of his place in the family. But the word of truth (which judges) and the word of grace (which accepts) must be heard together—as they were when the Word became flesh and dwelt among us in Jesus Christ.

4. Restoration is not a goal in itself. The restoration of the prodigal to his status as son and to his place in the family, as important as these are, did not represent the complete fulfillment of the father's purpose for the son. The younger son had yet to develop a style and quality of life that expressed that identity. In a similar way, the New Testament views the situation of believers. They have been restored to relation to the Father, have "put on the new self" (Colossians 3:10); but they have yet to develop fully the quality of life described as being "complete [i.e., mature] in Christ" (Colossians 1:28).

The restoration of the family still remained a goal at the end of the parable because of the intransigence of the older son. But in the event that the older son finally accepted the father's entreaty and the family was restored, there were yet other goals to be sought. Having the "kids under one roof" was not the final goal of the father. The quality of life that made for wholeness of the family must yet be developed. Likewise, the church as the family of God, even when restored to the identity that belongs to it as His gift and in accordance with His intention, still must develop a quality of life that embodies that identity. Paul, for example, never questions that the church of Corinth is a true church as respects its faith, ordinances, and the like; but he leaves no doubt that there is much to be desired in the quality of their life. In Ephesians 4:11-16, for another example, the appeal to a norm is the means to a still greater goal. The passage sounds a note of restoration: *speak the truth* (Ephesians 4:15). But the goal of this endeavor is that the Christian community might attain "unity of the faith, and of the knowledge of the Son of God, to a mature man," growing up "in all aspects into . . . Christ." In this way the body becomes a fit instrument for still yet another goal—of carrying out His will in the world (Ephesians 4:13, 15; cf. Ephesians 3:10, 11).

How inadequate is a concept of restoration that assumes that once there has been a recovery of the New Testament structure for initiation, worship, discipline, fellowship, and perhaps others, that the goal has been reached. The restored son still has goals to strive for. The restored family of God still has goals to strive for, both in the quality of its life and in its stewardship of the gospel. Such was the burden of Jesus' prayer on the eve of the crucifixion—that those who were drawn to Him in faith through the word of the apostles might be one, "that the world may believe" (John 17:20, 21).

NOTES

[1]A. M. Hunter, *The Parables Then and Now* (1971), p. 59.

[2]Dan Otto Via, Jr., *The Parables, Their Literary and Existential Dimension* (1967), pp. 11, 12; Hunter, *Parables Then and Now*, p. 11.

[3]Helmut Thielicke, *The Waiting Father Sermons on the Parables of Jesus* (1959), pp. 17, 18.

[4]Hunter, *Parables Then and Now*, p. 10.

[5]Ibid., p. 59.

[6]Ibid.

[7]Joachim Jeremias, *Parables of Jesus.* (1962), p. 230.

[8]Thielicke, *Waiting Father*, p. 29.

[9]Via, *Parables*, p. 169.

[10]Langdon Gilkey, *Maker of Heaven and Earth* (1965), pp. 229-236.

[11]Thielicke, *Waiting Father*, p. 22.

[12]Ibid., p. 25.

[13]Hunter, *Parables Then and Now*, p. 59.

[14]A. T. Robertson, *Word Pictures of the New Testament* (1931), IV, p. 240.

[15]Thielicke, *Waiting Father*, p. 27.

[16]Barton W. Stone, "Autobiography," in John Rogers, *Cane Ridge Meeting House*, p. 150.

[17]Via, *Parables*, p. 168.

[18]Ibid., pp. 168-9.

[19]Third World Conference on *Faith and Order* (1953), pp. 61-62.

[20]Thomas Campbell, *Declaration and Address*, (Bethany Press, 1955), p. 35.

[21]Alexander Campbell, *Christian System* (Standard, n.d.), pp. 215-16.

[22]R. A. F. MacKenzie, *Faith and History* (1963), p. 23.

[23]Via, *Parables*, p. 165.

[24]Thielicke, *Waiting Father*, p. 29.

[25]Francois Bovon, *Exegesis* (1978), p. 57.

[26]Via, *Parables*, p. 172.

[27]Thielicke, *Waiting Father*, p. 33.

[28]Bovon, *Exegesis*, p. 203.

[29]Thielicke, *Waiting Father*, p. 39.

[30]Ibid., p. 40.

[31]Hunter, *Parables Then and Now*, p. 59.

[32]"The Predicament of the Christian Historian," C. T. McIntire, ed., *God, History, and Historian* (1977), p. 408.

SOME SUGGESTED READINGS

The following is a brief list of works that will be helpful to readers who wish to explore further any technical questions pertaining to the parable of the prodigal son or its interpretation.

Bovon, Francois, and Rouiller, Gregoire, *Exegesis: Problems of Method and Exegesis in Reading* (Genesis 22 and Luke 15), Pittsburg: 1978.

Bruce, A. B. *The Parabolic Teaching of Jesus*, London: 1882.

Dodd, C. H. *Parables of The Kingdom*, London: 1936.

Hunter, A. M. *The Parables Then and Now*, Philadelphia: 1971.

Jeremias, Joachim, *Parables of Jesus*, New York: 1962.

Kissinger, Warren S., *Parables of Jesus, History of Interpretation and Bibliography*, Meteuchen, NJ: 1979.

Linnemann, Eta, *Parables of Jesus, Introduction and Exposition*, London: 1966.

Manson, T. W., *Sayings of Jesus*, London: 1949.

Stein, Robert H., *An Introduction to the Parables of Jesus*, Philadelphia: 1981.

Thielicke, Helmut, *The Waiting Father: Sermons in the Parables of Jesus*, London: 1959.

Via, Dan Otto, Jr., *The Parables: Their Literary and Existential Dimension*, Philadelphia: 1967.